Inside and Outside

A Sesame Street Guessing Game

Marie-Therese Miller

Lerner Publications ◆ Minneapolis

Join your favorite *Sesame Street* friends in a guessing game and learn about words that describe where things are. In the **Sesame Street® Directional Words** series, learning is fun for everyone in the neighborhood—especially when you're with your fabulous, furry friends!

Sincerely,
The Editors at Sesame Workshop

Table of Contents

Inside and Outside... 4

Can You Guess?...... 8

Point It Out! 20
Picture Glossary........... 22
Read More 23
Index 24

Inside and Outside

The words **inside** and **outside** tell where something is.

> My toys are **outside** the toy box when I play with them. I put them **inside** the toy box when I clean up.

Inside means an object is in something. Crayons go inside the box when you aren't coloring.

Elmo loves to color.

Outside means an object is not in something. Crayons are outside the box when you are coloring.

Can You Guess?

Let's see if you can tell if something is **inside** or **outside**.

Here are one, two, three, four, FIVE questions about **inside** and **outside**!

It's fun to pretend.

Are these friends **inside** or **outside** the playhouse?

They are **outside** the playhouse.

My friends and I pretend the playhouse is a fairy-tale castle.

These friends are camping.

Are they **inside** or **outside** the tent?

The friends are **inside** the tent.

Elmo loves to go camping with his Mommy and Daddy.

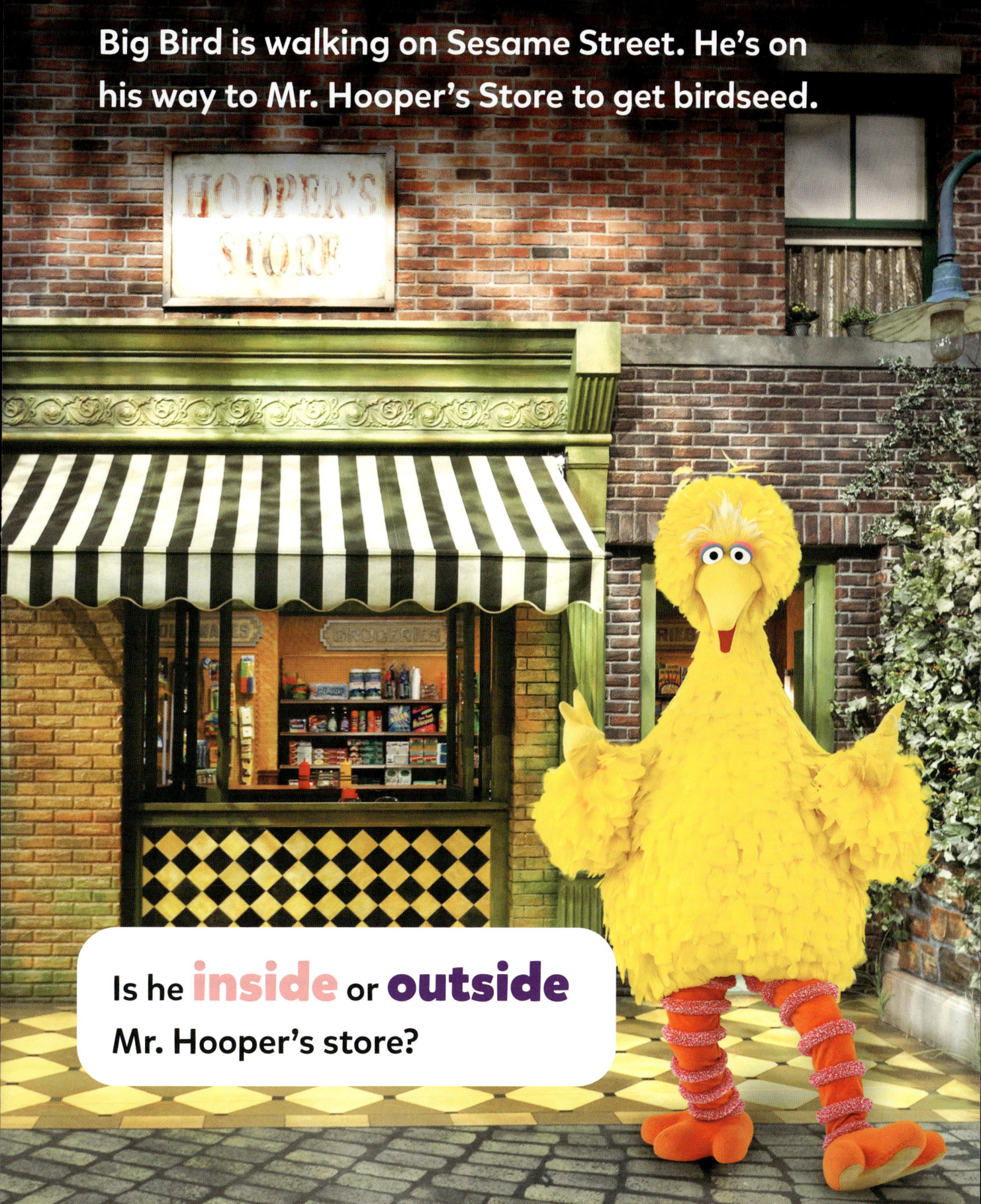

Big Bird is walking on Sesame Street. He's on his way to Mr. Hooper's Store to get birdseed.

Is he **inside** or **outside** Mr. Hooper's store?

Big Bird is **outside** Mr. Hooper's store.

I can't wait to make my birdseed smoothie!

It's time for school!

Is the food packed **inside** or **outside** the lunch box?

The food is packed **inside** the lunch box.

> What's your favorite thing to put **inside** your lunch box? I like carrots and hummus.

Ernie loves to play in the bathtub.

Is Ernie playing **inside** or **outside** the bathtub?

Ernie is playing **inside** the bathtub.

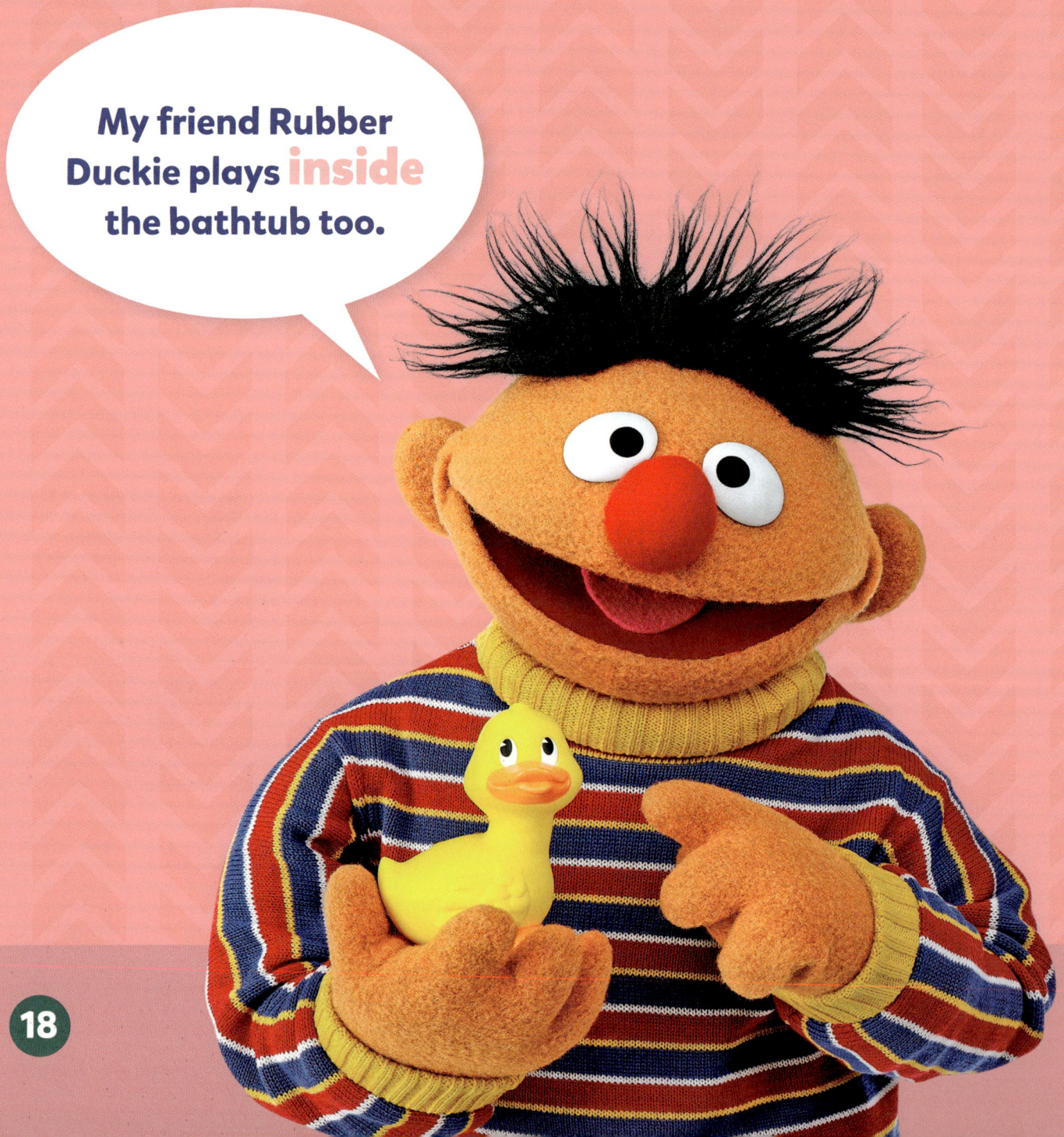

My friend Rubber Duckie plays inside the bathtub too.

Now you know all about **inside** and **outside**.

What are three things you see **inside** this room?

What are three things you see **outside** this window?

Point It Out!

Cookie Monster wants a cookie.

Me want cookies **inside** and **outside**!

Point to a cookie **inside** the cookie jar.
Point to a cookie **outside** the jar.

Picture Glossary

castle: a large home

hummus: a type of food made with mashed chickpeas and ground sesame seeds

skateboard: a small board with four wheels on the bottom

tent: a fabric shelter to protect people from the wind and rain

Read More

Culliford, Amy. *In and Out*. New York: Crabtree, 2022.

McDonnell, Rory. *In or Out?* New York: Gareth Stevens, 2020.

Miller, Marie-Therese. *Top and Bottom: A Sesame Street Guessing Game*. Minneapolis: Lerner Publications, 2024.

Index

bathtub, 17–18

crayons, 5–6

lunch box, 15–16

Mr. Hooper's Store, 13–14

playhouse, 9–10

tent, 11–12

Photo Acknowledgments

Image credits: JeepFoto/iStock/Getty Images, p. 5; monkeybusinessimages/iStock/Getty Images, p. 6; MachineHeadz/iStock/Getty Images, p. 9; FatCamera/E+/Getty Images, pp. 11, 22 (bottom right); Jose Luis Pelaez Inc/Digital Vision/Getty Images, p. 15; Ashok Sinha/DigitalVision/Getty Images, p. 19 (bottom); New Africa/Shutterstock, p. 19 (top); Aasthik Shanbhag/Shutterstock, p. 21; Natalia Klenova/Shutterstock, p. 22 (top right); Heike Brauer/Shutterstock, p. 22 (bottom left); VOJTa Herout/Shutterstock, p. 22 (top left). Cover: Fiona Jackson-Downes and Dirk Lindner/Image Source/Getty Images (right); somdul/Shutterstock (left).

To John, Meghan, John Vincent, Erin, Elizabeth, Michelle, and Greyson, beautiful inside and outside

Copyright © 2024 Sesame Workshop®, Sesame Street®, and associated characters, trademarks, and design elements are owned and licensed by Sesame Workshop. All rights reserved.

International copyright secured. No part of this book may be reproduced, stored in a retrieval system, or transmitted in any form or by any means—electronic, mechanical, photocopying, recording, or otherwise—without the prior written permission of Lerner Publishing Group, Inc., except for the inclusion of brief quotations in an acknowledged review.

Lerner Publications Company
An imprint of Lerner Publishing Group, Inc.
241 First Avenue North
Minneapolis, MN 55401 USA

For reading levels and more information, look up this title at www.lernerbooks.com.

Main body text set in Mikado.
Typeface provided by HVD.

Editor: Amber Ross **Designer:** Laura Otto Rinne

Library of Congress Cataloging-in-Publication Data

Names: Miller, Marie-Therese, author.
Title: Inside and outside : a Sesame Street guessing game / Marie-Therese Miller.
Description: Minneapolis : Lerner Publications, [2024] | Series: Sesame Street directional words | Audience: Ages 4–8 | Audience: Grades K–1 | Summary: "Join the friends from Sesame Street as they explore the concepts of inside and outside. Ample examples and a guessing game make this a fun and interactive learning experience for early learners"– Provided by publisher.
Identifiers: LCCN 2022035577 (print) | LCCN 2022035578 (ebook) | ISBN 9781728486741 (library binding) | ISBN 9798765601075 (ebook)
Subjects: LCSH: Guessing games—Juvenile literature. | Orientation—Juvenile literature.
Classification: LCC GV1473 .M55 2024 (print) | LCC GV1473 (ebook) | DDC 793.7–dc23/eng/20220811

LC record available at https://lccn.loc.gov/2022035577
LC ebook record available at https://lccn.loc.gov/2022035578

Manufactured in the United States of America
1-52619-50793-12/28/2022